T0400925

DiSNEY

BY HEATHER C. MORRIS

Apex is distributed by North Star Editions:
sales@northstareditions.com | 888-417-0195

Produced for Apex by Red Line Editorial.

Photographs ©: Rick Han/Pexels, cover; Walt Disney Pictures/Photofest, 1, 16–17; Patrick Connolly/Orlando Sentinel/TNS/Newscom, 4–5; Charles Sykes/Invision/AP Images, 6–7; Luis Santana/Tampa Bay Times/ZUMA Press/Newscom, 8; Shutterstock Images, 9, 13, 18, 19, 21, 22–23, 24, 25, 29; Harris & Ewing/Library of Congress, 10–11; Allstar Picture Library Ltd/Alamy, 12; iStockphoto, 14–15, 26–27; Walt Disney Studios Motion Pictures/Photofest, 20

Library of Congress Control Number: 2022920695

ISBN
978-1-63738-564-7 (hardcover)
978-1-63738-618-7 (paperback)
978-1-63738-721-4 (ebook pdf)
978-1-63738-672-9 (hosted ebook)

Printed in the United States of America
Mankato, MN
082023

NOTE TO PARENTS AND EDUCATORS

Apex books are designed to build literacy skills in striving readers. Exciting, high-interest content attracts and holds readers' attention. The text is carefully leveled to allow students to achieve success quickly. Additional features, such as bolded glossary words for difficult terms, help build comprehension.

TABLE OF CONTENTS

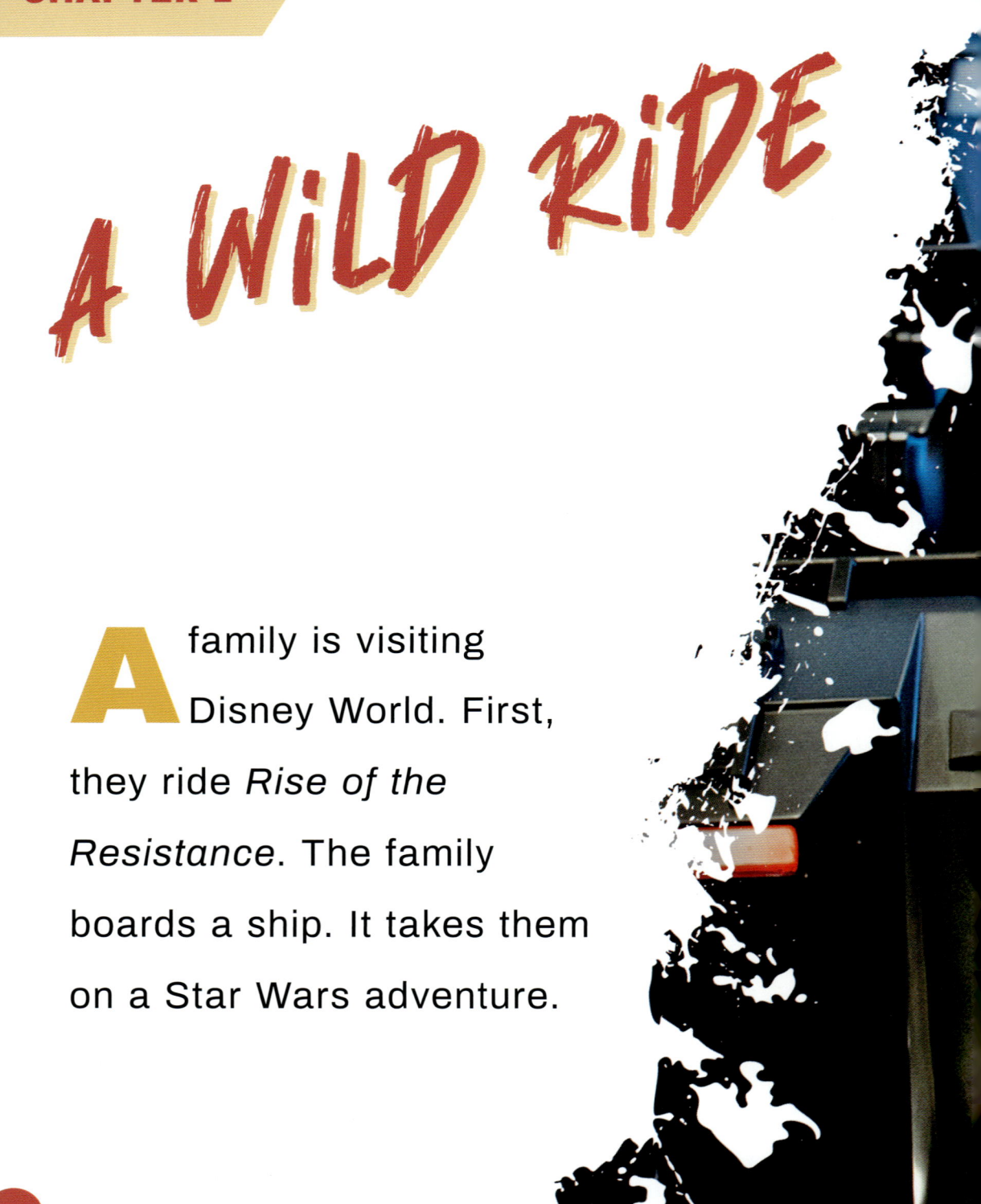

CHAPTER 1

A WILD RIDE

A family is visiting Disney World. First, they ride *Rise of the Resistance*. The family boards a ship. It takes them on a Star Wars adventure.

In *Rise of the Resistance*, a droid rides with each ship.

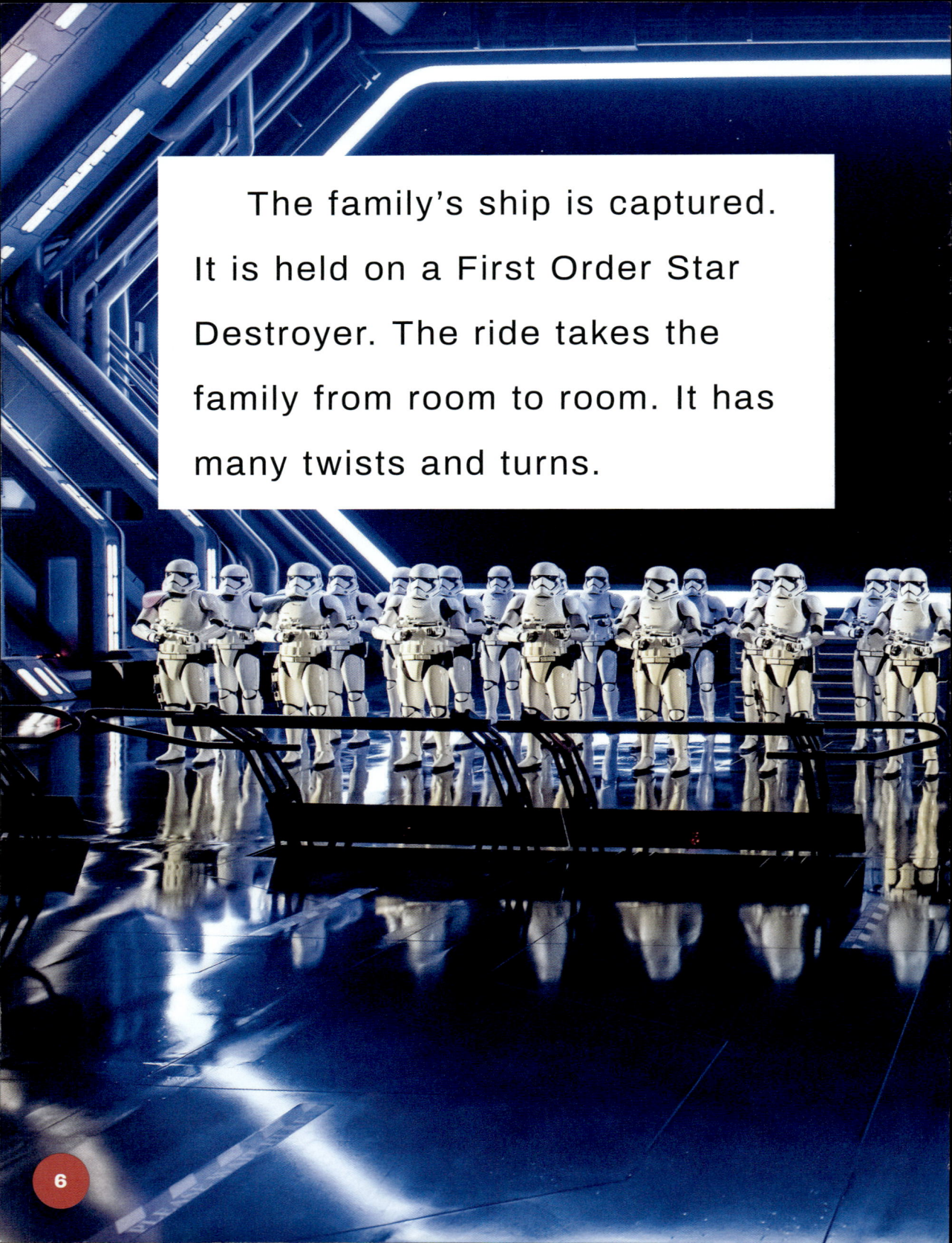

The family's ship is captured. It is held on a First Order Star Destroyer. The ride takes the family from room to room. It has many twists and turns.

Riders see many stormtroopers during *Rise of the Resistance*.

The ship escapes. A video shows it flying through space. It makes a rough landing. But the family is safe.

Riders meet several Star Wars characters, including Rey.

Disney's first Star Wars movie was *The Force Awakens*. It came out in 2015.

STAR WARS

The first Star Wars movie came out in 1977. Fans loved it. In 2012, Disney bought the company. By 2022, there were 12 Star Wars movies and several TV shows.

CHAPTER 2

DISNEY HISTORY

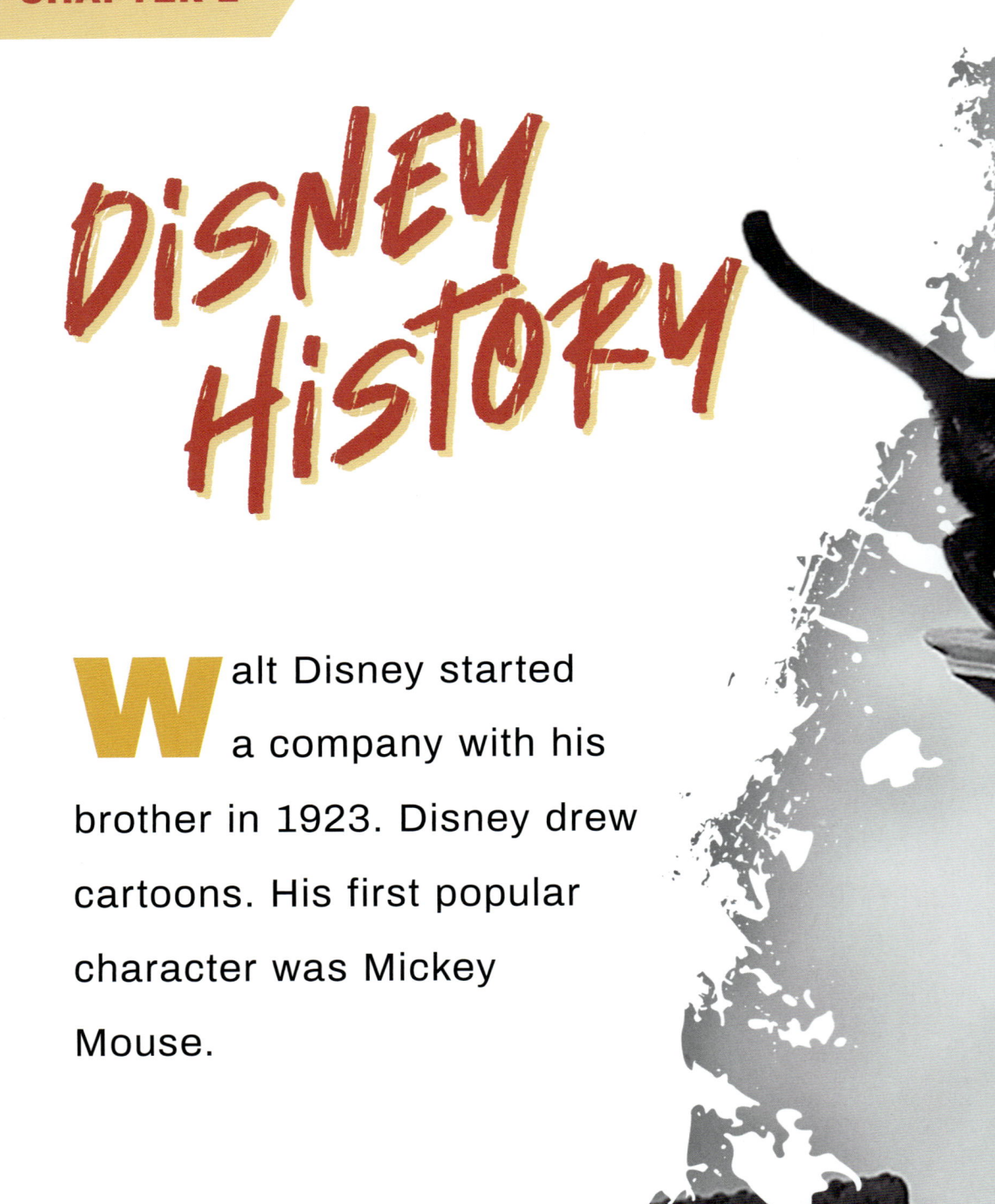

Walt Disney started a company with his brother in 1923. Disney drew cartoons. His first popular character was Mickey Mouse.

Walt Disney poses with a drawing of Mickey Mouse in 1931.

Snow White and the Seven Dwarfs is based on an old fairy tale.

In 1937, Disney released its first **feature film**. It was called *Snow White and the Seven Dwarfs*. Audiences packed theaters to see it.

POPULAR EARLY MOVIES

Disney became known for its **animated** movies. *Pinocchio* was the company's second big hit. *Dumbo* and *Bambi* came after. *Cinderella* came out in 1950.

Pinocchio is about a puppet who tries to become a real boy.

13

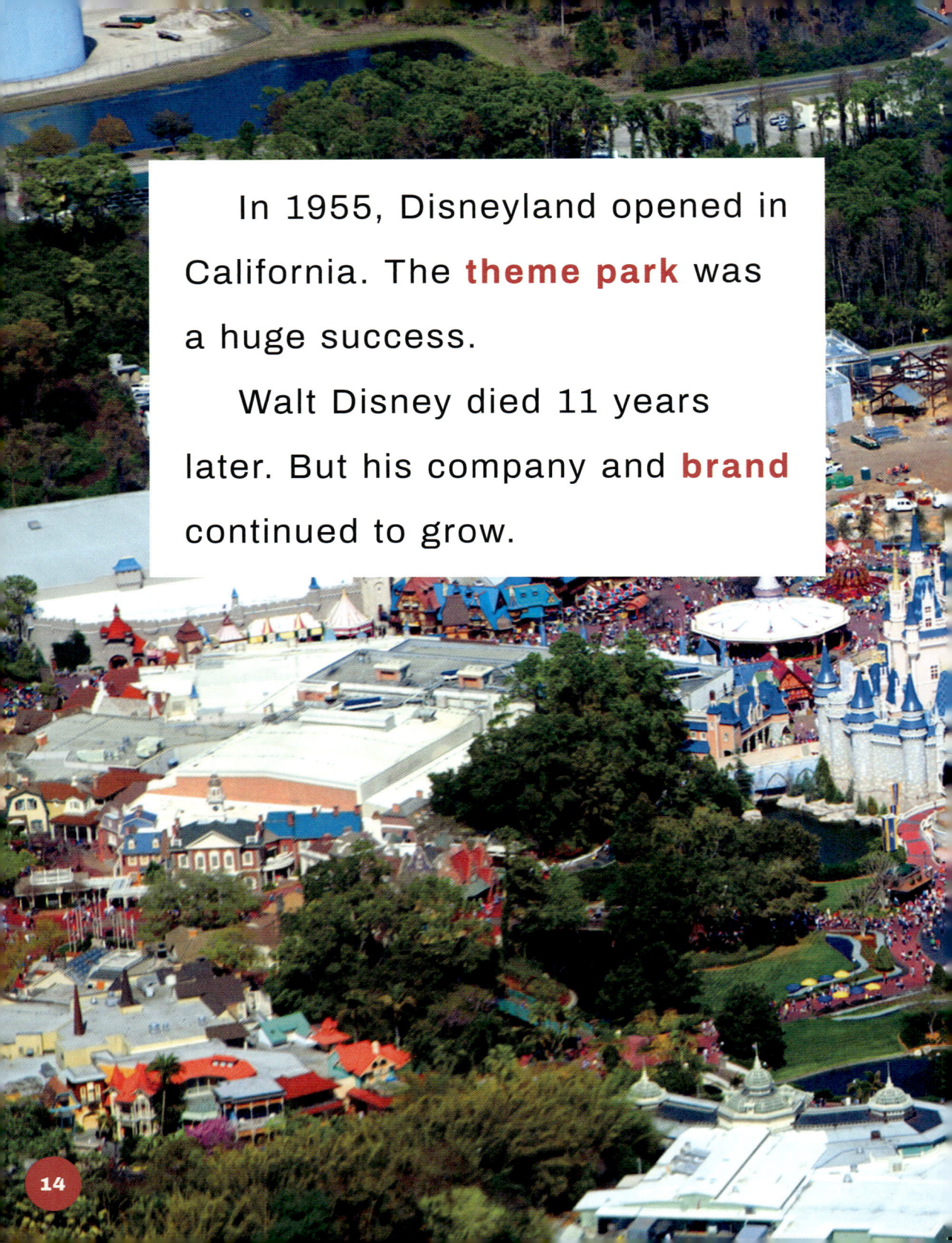

In 1955, Disneyland opened in California. The **theme park** was a huge success.

Walt Disney died 11 years later. But his company and **brand** continued to grow.

FAST FACT

In 1971, a second Disney theme park opened in Florida. It was Walt Disney World.

Walt Disney World is nearly the same size as San Francisco, California.

CHAPTER 3

GROWING THE MAGIC

In 1989, Disney released *The Little Mermaid*. More hit movies followed. *Beauty and the Beast*, *Aladdin*, and *The Lion King* won many awards.

The Lion King came out in 1994.

In 2006, Disney expanded. Pixar joined the company. Later, Disney bought Marvel Studios and Star Wars.

Pixar's *Toy Story* was the first animated movie made entirely with computers.

+ Abberation, Particles, Glow, Depth of Field

Tens of thousands of people work as computer animators in the United States.

FAST FACT

Early animated movies used illustrations. People drew each **frame** by hand. Pixar uses computers instead.

Encanto came out in 2021.

Disney kept making popular movies. *Frozen*, *Moana*, and *Encanto* all had hit songs. In 2019, the company started Disney+. This **streaming service** lets people watch online.

NO. 1 SONG

"We Don't Talk About Bruno" appeared in *Encanto*. In 2022, the song reached No. 1 on the *Billboard* Hot 100 charts. It was the first Disney song to do so in nearly 30 years.

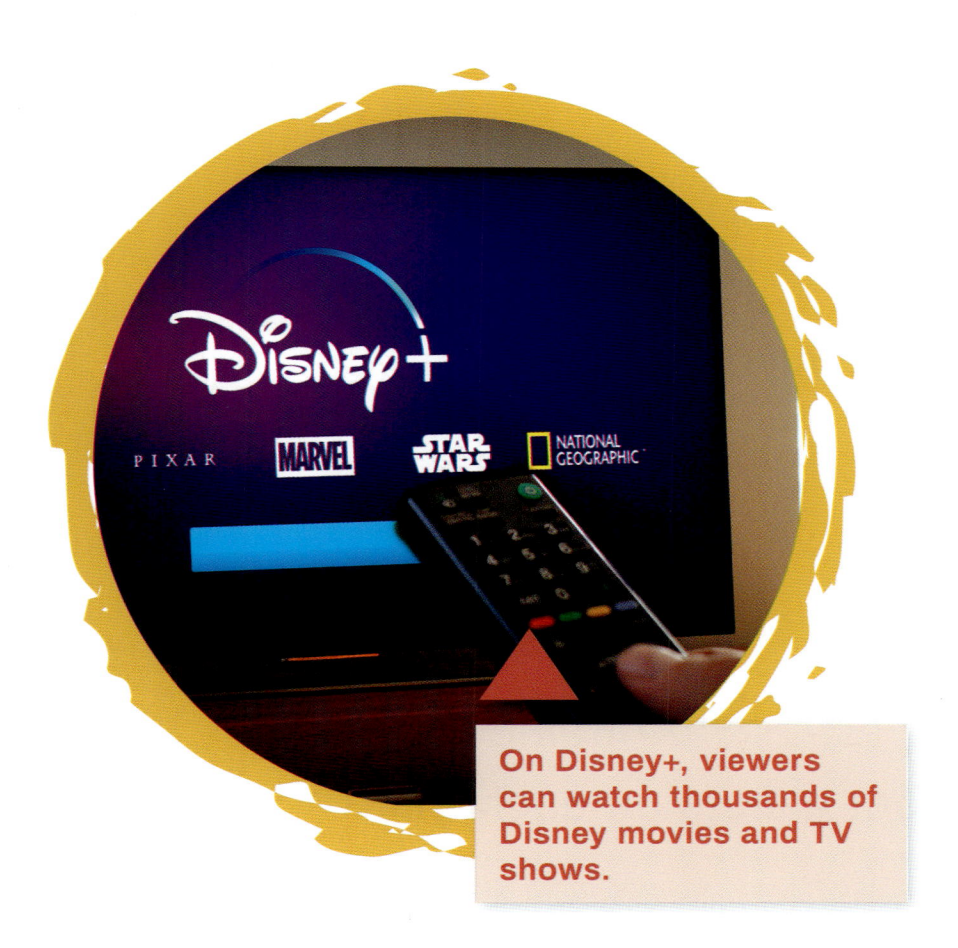

On Disney+, viewers can watch thousands of Disney movies and TV shows.

CHAPTER 4

MAGICAL EXPERIENCES

The Disney brand includes more than movies. For example, it offers vacations. Disney's **cruise ships** sail to many places. Disney characters greet guests on each trip.

Disney cruise ships can hold thousands of people.

Disney also has its own TV channel. Disney Channel plays many shows and movies. It has helped many actors become famous.

Zendaya is a popular actor. She got her start on Disney Channel in the early 2010s.

Disney sometimes teams up with other brands. For example, LEGO has Disney-themed sets.

MANY PRODUCTS

Disney is known for its **merchandise**. It makes and sells clothes, toys, and more. People can also buy Disney games and **decorations**. The company even has its own stores.

Rides light up at night at Disneyland in Anaheim, California.

Disney has theme parks around the world. They feature rides and roller coasters. Visitors meet their favorite characters, too. Disney keeps giving fans new experiences to enjoy.

COMPREHENSION
QUESTIONS

Write your answers on a separate piece of paper.

1. Write a few sentences describing some of the things other than movies that Disney makes.

2. Which Disney character is your favorite? Why?

3. What was Walt Disney's first feature film?

    A. *Snow White and the Seven Dwarfs*

    B. *Cinderella*

    C. *The Lion King*

4. Which Disney movie featured a No. 1 song?

    A. *Frozen*

    B. *The Little Mermaid*

    C. *Encanto*

5. What does **illustrations** mean in this book?

*Early animated movies used **illustrations**. People drew each frame by hand.*

    A. animal actors

    B. drawings

    C. real-life events

6. What does **performances** mean in this book?

*People can see **performances** based on Disney movies. These include plays and ice-skating shows.*

    A. ways that computers make movies

    B. toys that companies make and sell

    C. events where people act, sing, or play for a group

Answer key on page 32.

29

GLOSSARY

animated
Made from many images shown one after another.

brand
The products and services connected with one company.

cruise ships
Large ships that people travel on for fun.

decorations
Things that make a place look more beautiful and fun.

feature film
A movie telling a story that is usually over 80 minutes long.

frame
One picture in a movie.

merchandise
Products sold by a certain company.

streaming service
An online source where users watch video using the internet.

theme park
A fun place filled with rides and games that are based on one idea, story, or brand.

TO LEARN MORE

BOOKS

Klepeis, Alicia Z. *Walt Disney*. Minneapolis: Abdo Publishing, 2022.

Schwartz, Heather E. *Zendaya: Hollywood Superstar*. Minneapolis: Lerner Publications, 2023.

Walter Foster Jr. Creative Team. *Learn to Draw Disney·Pixar: Toy Story, Favorite Characters*. Mission Viejo, CA: Walter Foster Jr., 2020.

ONLINE RESOURCES

Visit **www.apexeditions.com** to find links and resources related to this title.

ABOUT THE AUTHOR

Heather C. Morris writes books for kids who love science and imagination. Her favorite Disney princess is Belle. Her favorite Disney World ride is *Seven Dwarfs Mine Train*.

INDEX

ANSWER KEY:
1. Answers will vary; 2. Answers will vary; 3. A; 4. C; 5. B; 6. C